K Curran

shika, shika

Mincyambo / Botanas

Yeahman

SELF-CARE

*How to live mindfully
and look after yourself*

CLAIRE CHAMBERLAIN

SELF-CARE

An Hachette UK Company
www.hachette.co.uk

Vie Books, an imprint of Summersdale Publishers Ltd
Part of Octopus Publishing Group Limited
Carmelite House
50 Victoria Embankment
LONDON
EC4Y 0DZ
UK

www.summersdale.com

Printed and bound in China

ISBN: 978-1-78685-775-0

Substantial discounts on bulk quantities of Summersdale books are available to corporations, professional associations and other organizations. For details contact general enquiries: telephone: +44 (0) 1243 771107 or email: enquiries@summersdale.com.

INTRODUCTION

If you often find yourself feeling "burnt out" by the pressures and strains of everyday life, it could be time to introduce a little self-care into your daily routine. Despite the name, self-care is certainly not selfish – it simply means taking steps toward looking after your own mental, emotional, spiritual and physical well-being. This book is packed full of practical, easy-to-adopt tips and inspiring quotations to help enrich the most intimate and long-lasting relationship in your life – the one you have with yourself.

Self-care means
giving yourself
permission
to pause.

Cecilia Tran

BE CLEAR ON SELF-CARE

When looking to care for yourself more fully, it's important to understand what "self-care" means. The term refers to any deliberate act you undertake that protects and nurtures your own physical, mental, emotional and spiritual health. It doesn't just entail pampering. Instead, self-care encompasses a number of practices, from eating healthily and exercising to becoming more mindful and embracing meditation, which can relieve stress and anxiety, while nourishing your body and soul.

IT'S NOT
SELFISH TO
LOVE YOURSELF,
TAKE CARE OF
YOURSELF, AND
TO MAKE YOUR
HAPPINESS A
PRIORITY. IT'S
NECESSARY.

MANDY HALE

Let go of guilt

Often the biggest barrier to self-care is guilt. Feeling bad about spending time tending to your own needs is common, especially if you feel you should be caring for someone else or doing something that appears outwardly more productive. But remember, taking time to look after your own mental and physical well-being will ultimately leave you with more reserves of energy to invest in others, not less. It's time to drop the guilt and recognize self-care as a wholly necessary, healthy and vital act.

Carve out and

claim the time to

care for yourself

and kindle your own

fire.

Amy Ippoliti

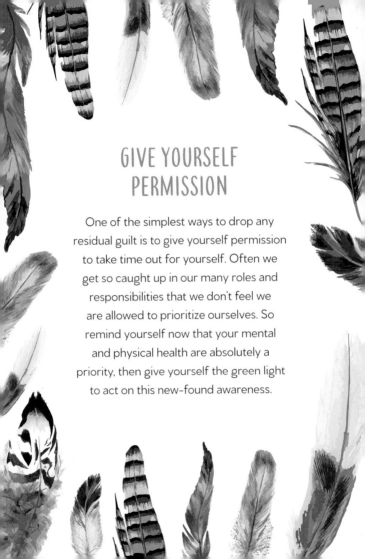

GIVE YOURSELF PERMISSION

One of the simplest ways to drop any residual guilt is to give yourself permission to take time out for yourself. Often we get so caught up in our many roles and responsibilities that we don't feel we are allowed to prioritize ourselves. So remind yourself now that your mental and physical health are absolutely a priority, then give yourself the green light to act on this new-found awareness.

Rest and
self-care are
so important...
You can not
serve from an
empty vessel.

Eleanor Brownn

Love yourself
enough to set
boundaries. Your
time and energy
are precious.
You get to choose
how you use it.

Anna Taylor

SCHEDULE SOME "ME TIME"

With all of the other daily tasks you need to complete, it's easy to demote yourself to the bottom of your to-do list. So schedule some time for self-care each day – physically writing it down in your diary, or setting an online reminder, means you will be more likely to follow through with your intention.

Some days you may find a whole hour or evening for self-care, while on others five minutes to sit quietly and focus may be all you get. No matter how little time you have, block it out in your diary, to ensure the moment doesn't get swallowed up by everyday chores and other responsibilities.

Self-care is
never selfish, but it
may feel that way
when you live a
frenzied life.

ARTHUR P. CIARAMICOLI

TIME YOU ENJOY WASTING IS NOT WASTED TIME.

MARTHE TROLY-CURTIN

FINDING THE TIME

Figure out the moments of the day when you can make time for yourself. Even if you have a packed schedule, there will be pockets of time to set aside for self-care. Early mornings, lunch breaks and evenings are common times of the day when you might have some alone time. Think also about times where you're simply waiting –

waiting for a train, for food to cook in the oven, or for your child's after-school activity to finish. These are perfect moments for self-care, such as getting lost in a book, going for a mindful stroll, sipping a hot cup of tea, or meditation – it can be whatever you fancy! Carve out these pockets of free time for yourself.

ALMOST EVERYTHING WILL WORK AGAIN IF YOU UNPLUG IT FOR A FEW MINUTES, INCLUDING YOU.

ANNE LAMOTT

Switch off each day

Being constantly connected in an "always-on" world can feel overwhelming sometimes. Even in your downtime, you might find yourself staring at screens, answering messages and getting sucked into social media. One of the simplest and easiest ways to recharge is to switch off, both physically and mentally: turn off or remove any electronic devices, close your eyes, take a series of deep breaths and allow yourself to tune into your senses.

WHEN YOU SAY
"YES" TO OTHERS,
MAKE SURE YOU
ARE NOT SAYING
"NO" TO YOURSELF.

PAULO COELHO

It's only by saying "no" that you can concentrate on the things that are really important.

STEVE JOBS

BECOME COMFORTABLE WITH "NO"

Saying "no" can be hard. We are often socialized to believe that refusing other people's requests for help is selfish. We worry we'll appear uncaring or, worse, damage our relationships. But what if, by saying yes, you're risking your own mental and physical health? The sad fact is that, in an effort to be liked, many of us take on additional chores, projects and responsibilities without pausing to consider how this will affect our well-being. Next time someone asks you for a favour, don't agree automatically. If you want to say no, be kind but firm, such as: "Thanks for asking, but I'm afraid I can't this evening." (Note that you don't have to justify your decision with a reason either!) Alternatively, if you aren't confident enough to be so direct, buy yourself time. Saying, "Let me check my diary and get back to you," allows you to step away from the situation and consider how the request will affect your own time and energy levels.

Saying yes to
happiness means
learning to say no to
the things and people
that stress you out.

Thema Bryant-Davis

Lighten up on yourself. No one is **perfect**. *Gently* accept your **humanness.**

Deborah Day

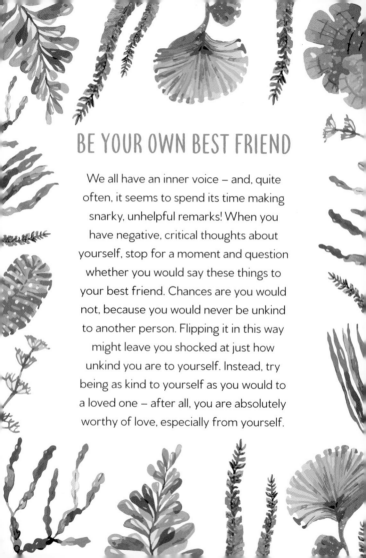

BE YOUR OWN BEST FRIEND

We all have an inner voice – and, quite often, it seems to spend its time making snarky, unhelpful remarks! When you have negative, critical thoughts about yourself, stop for a moment and question whether you would say these things to your best friend. Chances are you would not, because you would never be unkind to another person. Flipping it in this way might leave you shocked at just how unkind you are to yourself. Instead, try being as kind to yourself as you would to a loved one – after all, you are absolutely worthy of love, especially from yourself.

SELF-COMPASSION IS SIMPLY GIVING THE SAME KINDNESS TO OURSELVES THAT WE WOULD GIVE TO OTHERS.

CHRISTOPHER GERMER

Belonging is
not fitting in…
Belonging starts with
self-acceptance.

Brené Brown

Forgive yourself

Part of being kind to yourself is recognizing that everyone makes mistakes – they're a natural part of development. Next time things go wrong, don't be hard on yourself. Instead, accept what has happened. Make sure you are accountable and apologize if necessary, then forgive yourself fully. Learning from mistakes and moving on is far healthier than continually berating yourself and feeling forever guilty.

EMBRACE THE GLORIOUS MESS THAT YOU ARE.

ELIZABETH GILBERT

Be nice to yourself. It's hard to be happy when someone is mean to you all the time.

Christine Arylo

SWAP "SHOULD" FOR "COULD"

The vocabulary you use, even internally, plays a big role in how you view your responsibilities in life. Simply by switching the word "should" for "could" when talking about plans is a fantastic way of reducing the pressure you put on yourself. Telling yourself you "should" clear your work inbox is very different to telling yourself you "could" clear your work inbox: the latter ensures there's no guilt if it doesn't quite happen. Flexible plans are far better than setting yourself rigid structures that must be adhered to.

Seasons change, people grow together and apart, life moves on. You will be OK. Embrace it.

ALEXANDRA ELLE

How we care for
ourselves gives our brain
messages that shape our
self-worth, so we must
care for ourselves in
every way, every day.

SAM OWEN

The only person
who can pull me
down is myself, and
I'm not going to let
myself pull me
down any more.

C. JoyBell C.

REPEAT POSITIVE AFFIRMATIONS

As awkward as it can feel when you first start, positive
self-talk is a wonderful way to cancel out any limiting
beliefs that might be hanging around in your mind. The
key to affirmations is in repetition: if you repeat them
often enough, they will become beliefs, and once you
believe these powerful statements about yourself, it will
have a profoundly positive impact on your life. Positive
affirmations should mean something to you, so choose
to say something you want to start believing about

yourself, or something that reflects how you wish to lead your life. Examples could be "I choose to feel happy in my mind, body and soul"; "I am adventurous, fearless and free"; "I am perfect exactly as I am"; "I forgive past mistakes and live mindfully in the present moment"; or "I am beautiful, unique and interesting". Take care to use the present tense and phrase them positively rather than negatively ("I am" rather than "I am not"). Once you've honed your personalized affirmations, say them aloud to yourself several times a day. You could even write them down and leave them where you will see them often, such as on your bedside table or bathroom mirror. Your affirmations will soon become your reality as you begin to believe in them fully.

KEEP A GRATITUDE JOURNAL

Take a few moments to write down the things you are grateful for each day. Many of us take our blessings for granted, or get so caught up in our daily lives that we never stop to appreciate what we have. By listing three or more things you're grateful for daily, from hugging a loved one to a delicious home-cooked meal, you will become fully conscious of all the ways you are fortunate – an experience that can make you feel instantly happier.

Change your
thoughts and you
change your world.

Norman Vincent Peale

DON'T AIM FOR PERFECTION

Do you sometimes find yourself striving for perfection, feeling that you will only be worthy once you have become the "perfect" student/employee/colleague/parent? The problem with perfection is it's a state that's impossible to attain. If this is what you're aiming for, you will find yourself consistently falling short of your own high expectations, which can leave you feeling dejected and as though you have failed. It's time to let the idea of perfection go. Still try your best, of course, but realize that being "good enough" truly is good enough. This way, you can never fail. Adopting this mindset also frees you up to try new hobbies, start new friendships or relationships; or go for that promotion: suddenly you don't have to be the best, you simply have to try your best, and if it doesn't work out, you can just try your best somewhere else, knowing that you are perfect exactly as you are... imperfections and all!

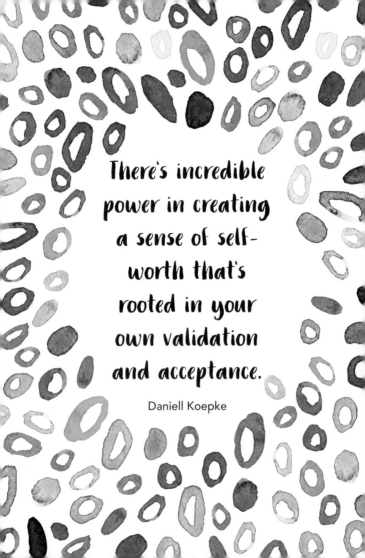

There's incredible power in creating a sense of self-worth that's rooted in your own validation and acceptance.

Daniell Koepke

Nobody's perfect, so give yourself credit for everything you're doing right, and be kind to yourself when you struggle.

Lori Deschene

Be thankful for what you have; you'll end up having more. If you concentrate on what you don't have, you will never, ever have enough.

OPRAH WINFREY

I THINK HAPPINESS IS
A CHOICE. IF YOU FEEL
YOURSELF BEING HAPPY
AND CAN SETTLE IN TO
THE LIFE CHOICES YOU
MAKE, THEN IT'S GREAT.

DREW BARRYMORE

Smile more

While it doesn't seem very natural to give a big cheesy grin when you're in a bad mood or feeling low, smiling on purpose can actually help to lift your mood and make you feel better. The reason? The very act of smiling alters your brain chemistry, prompting the release of the feel-good neurotransmitters serotonin, dopamine and endorphins. So even when you're worried, anxious or stressed, try a smile and the good mood may follow. As the saying goes, fake it till you make it!

LAUGHTER IS AN INSTANT VACATION.

MILTON BERLE

HAVE A LAUGH!

There's nothing quite like a heartfelt belly laugh to boost your sense of well-being. In fact, studies have shown that laughing triggers the release of endorphins in the body. What's more, laughter has also been shown to lower blood pressure and increase antibody production, which improves your ability to fight infection and disease. So make time to watch your favourite comedy or listen to a funny podcast – you'll be doing your mind and body a favour and having fun while you're at it!

Laughter is the *tonic*,

the *relief*,

the *surcease*

for *pain*.

Charlie Chaplin

CHAT WITH A FRIEND

You might be surprised by just how good it feels to have a long natter with a friend, especially if you haven't been in touch for a while. Opening up to a loved one is truly cathartic, so make time to connect properly with someone you care about. If you're feeling low or

depressed, it might seem difficult to start talking to a friend or family member about how you're feeling, but take comfort in the fact that many people report feeling much better after sharing their thoughts and experiences. If you don't feel up to talking to a friend, either in person or on the phone, why not send them a text message to let them know how you're doing?

WE SET THE STANDARD
FOR HOW WE WANT
TO BE TREATED. OUR
RELATIONSHIPS ARE
A REFLECTION OF THE
RELATIONSHIP WE HAVE
WITH OURSELVES.

IYANLA VANZANT

The present
moment is filled
with joy and
happiness. If
you are attentive,
you will see it.

THÍCH NHẤT HẠNH

BECOME MORE MINDFUL

Mindfulness simply means becoming aware of the present moment: calmly noticing any thoughts, feelings or bodily sensations you may be experiencing, but without making any judgement. It's a way of reconnecting with your body, and the world around you, without the worries which stop you experiencing the present fully and consciously. Ensuring you are present and aware of the moment – whether you're performing breathing techniques, meditating, eating delicious food or sipping a cup of tea – will help you experience it more deeply, heightening your sense of fulfilment and relaxation. Drawing your attention to the present moment sounds simple, but it can take a little practice, so don't worry if you struggle at first. As soon as you notice a thought or emotion arise that takes your mind away from the present moment, acknowledge it without judgement, and then simply draw your attention back to the "now".

Although the world
is full of suffering,
it is full also of the
overcoming of it.

Helen Keller

Let go of the *past,*

let go of the *future.*

Let go of the

present.

Buddha

PRACTISE MEDITATION

Meditation is essentially focused attention. It can have a wonderfully calming effect, helping you to recharge and leaving you with a greater sense of well-being and increased energy. You could try to set aside a little time each day when you will not be disturbed, such as early morning, to meditate. To begin, ensure you're sitting comfortably, either on a chair or cross-legged on a cushion. Keep your back straight and upright, and gently

close your eyes. There are many
different meditation techniques,
some of which focus on breathing,
others that entail becoming aware of
bodily sensations or focusing your
full attention on an external object.
Whichever you decide to try, aim to
clear your mind of all other thoughts
or emotions. If you notice thoughts
creeping back in, simply draw your
mind back to the focus of your
attention, without guilt or judgement.
Aim for just ten minutes daily to
begin with – even a short session
can make a big difference to your
physical and emotional health.

Wherever
you are,
be there
totally.

Eckhart Tolle

SURRENDER
TO WHAT IS.
LET GO OF
WHAT WAS.
HAVE FAITH
IN WHAT
WILL BE.

SONIA RICOTTI

PERFORM A "BODY SCAN"

A body scan meditation is a wonderful way to become fully aware of your body in the present moment and, while relaxation is not the end goal, it's a common side effect. To begin, sit or lie in a comfortable position, loosening any tight clothing so you don't experience constriction. Take a few deep breaths to prepare yourself for the meditation, then start to bring your awareness to your feet: pay attention to the weight of them on the floor, note any sensations such as pain, warmth or coolness, tension or ease.

The aim is not to judge or change how your body is feeling, but simply to notice. Next, move your awareness slowly up your body, scanning your legs, buttocks, hips, pelvis, lower back, stomach, chest, upper back, shoulders, arms, hands, fingers, neck, jaw, cheeks, eyes, forehead and temples, noting how each body part feels in that moment. Bringing awareness, as opposed to thoughts, into your body is very grounding and can instil a sense of peace. There is no time limit on a body scan – you could try it for five minutes at first. You can also find guided body scan meditations online.

TRY REIKI

The term "reiki" is derived from the Japanese
words *rei* (meaning "universal") and *ki*
(meaning "life energy"), and is an alternative
therapy commonly known as energy healing.
It is said to involve the transfer of universal
energy from the practitioner's palms to the
patient's body and, while its effectiveness
is hard to prove in scientific terms, many
who receive reiki are convinced it works.
Reiki aims to increase your life-force energy,
which in turn improves physical, mental
and spiritual well-being, promotes healing,
aids relaxation, relieves stress and invokes a
feeling of deep peace – perfect for self-care.

He who lives in
harmony with himself
lives in harmony
with the universe.

Marcus Aurelius

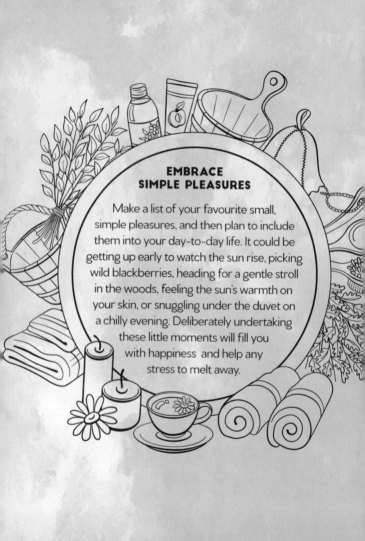

EMBRACE
SIMPLE PLEASURES

Make a list of your favourite small, simple pleasures, and then plan to include them into your day-to-day life. It could be getting up early to watch the sun rise, picking wild blackberries, heading for a gentle stroll in the woods, feeling the sun's warmth on your skin, or snuggling under the duvet on a chilly evening. Deliberately undertaking these little moments will fill you with happiness and help any stress to melt away.

Every act of self-care
is a powerful declaration:
I am on my side.

Susan Weiss Berry

Seek out activities that make you happy

Partaking in activities that make you happy should definitely be on your weekly to-do list! Think about all the people, places and hobbies that make you feel great – it could be spending time with a close friend, visiting the coast, exercising, baking or camping. Then try to ensure you incorporate these activities into your everyday life whenever possible.

THE MOST SIMPLE THINGS CAN BRING THE MOST HAPPINESS.

IZABELLA SCORUPCO

TREAT YOURSELF

Treating yourself for no reason is guaranteed to put a spring in your step and a smile on your face. You don't need to splash out lots of cash, either (indeed, that could be counterproductive!) – why not buy yourself a bunch of your favourite flowers, that novel you can't wait to read, or a new accessory in your favourite colour?

If your **compassion**

does not **include**

yourself. it is

incomplete.

Jack Kornfield

Meditation can
help us embrace
our worries, our fear,
our anger; and that
is very healing.

Thích Nhất Hạnh

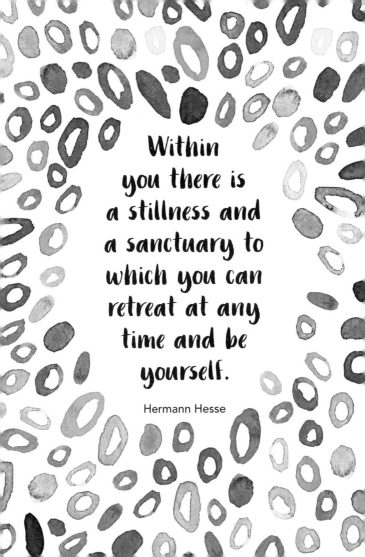

Within you there is a stillness and a sanctuary to which you can retreat at any time and be yourself.

Hermann Hesse

Have a massage

Investing in a massage is a wonderful way to care for yourself. Not only can it promote a deep sense of relaxation throughout the whole body, but it has also been proven to ease stress, alleviate depression, improve circulation, soothe away pain, relieve digestive disorders and lead to a better night's sleep – perfect for calming your mind, body and soul.

TENSION
IS WHO YOU
THINK YOU
SHOULD BE.
RELAXATION
IS WHO
YOU ARE.

CHINESE PROVERB

Solitude is
creativity's best
friend, and solitude
is refreshment
for our souls.

Naomi Judd

SPEND TIME
ALONE EACH DAY

There is a big difference between feeling
lonely and spending time alone. A little
solitude each day is a wonderful way to
quieten your mind, still your thoughts and
reconnect with yourself. What's more,
research now shows that time alone
helps to increase empathy, productivity,
creativity and mental resilience. So
take a moment to yourself each day,
however short, and enjoy the peace.

SOLITUDE
HAS ITS OWN
VERY STRANGE
BEAUTY.

LIV TYLER

SOMETIMES
YOU JUST
HAVE TO STOP,
TAKE A DEEP
BREATH AND
PUT THINGS IN
PERSPECTIVE.

KATRINA MAYER

BREATHE MORE DEEPLY

Taking the time to breathe consciously and deeply, also known as diaphragmatic breathing, is a centuries-old technique that helps to relieve anxiety and stress, making it a perfect self-care practice. The beauty of performing breathwork is that it can be done virtually anywhere and you don't need lots of time, so it's a wonderful way to introduce self-care into each and every day. To begin,

simply ensure you're sitting comfortably in a peaceful setting, then start to breathe consciously, focusing on elongating each inhale through your nose, feeling your belly expand and rise, and then exhaling for the same length of time. The scientific reason behind why it's such a powerful way to unwind lies in the fact that breathing deeply interrupts the body's "fight or flight" response, instead triggering relaxation.

Sometimes the most
important thing in
a whole day is the
rest we take between
two deep breaths.

Etty Hillesum

I felt my lungs inflate

with the onrush of scenery –

air, mountains,

trees, people.

I thought, "This is what it is to be

happy."

Sylvia Plath

CONNECT WITH NATURE

Spending time in the natural world can have an impressive restorative effect on both your mind and body – in fact, numerous scientific studies point to the fact that being outside in nature can help to ease stress, fight anxiety and depression, reduce inflammation, improve short-term memory, lower blood pressure, boost your immune system and spark your creativity. So get out there whenever you can: stroll through woodland, walk barefoot on the grass, hug a tree, take a dip in the sea, grow a plant from seed – whatever takes your fancy!

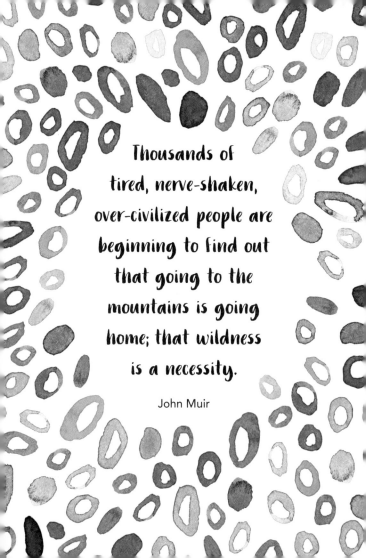

Thousands of
tired, nerve-shaken,
over-civilized people are
beginning to find out
that going to the
mountains is going
home; that wildness
is a necessity.

John Muir

We need the
tonic of wildness...
We can never have
enough of nature.

Henry David Thoreau

People who love themselves come across as very loving, generous and kind; they express their self-confidence through humility, forgiveness and inclusiveness.

SANAYA ROMAN

GET SOME SUNSHINE

While getting too much sun is detrimental to your health, exposing you to ultraviolet rays that put you at risk of skin cancer, heading outside in natural daylight is important for your well-being. As well as making vitamin D directly via sunshine, your body produces more mood-boosting serotonin when exposed to sunlight, helping to make you feel happier and more alert. Aim for 15 minutes outside in the sunshine each day whenever possible, with your face, arms and hands exposed, to gain maximum benefit. These short bursts are especially important during the autumn and winter months, when reduced daylight hours and long, dark evenings can make you feel tired and lethargic.

EXERCISE IS AMAZING, FROM THE INSIDE OUT. I FEEL SO ALIVE AND HAVE MORE ENERGY.

VANESSA HUDGENS

To enjoy the glow of
good health, you
must exercise.

Gene Tunney

FIND A WORKOUT YOU ENJOY

Taking care of your physical health is of the utmost importance, so try to incorporate exercise into your daily routine. Current guidelines recommend 150 minutes of exercise each week (that's just 30 minutes, five times a week), and it should be brisk enough to raise your heart rate. Exercise offers a whole host of physical benefits, including improved fitness, weight management, and lowering your risk of heart disease, type 2 diabetes, high cholesterol and stroke. But there's more... physical activity promotes the release of endorphins into your bloodstream, which boosts your mood, lowers stress and eases depression. So get moving! Don't fancy sweating it out in a gym? That's fine. It's important to choose an exercise you enjoy, so you have fun and stick with it. There are so many options, including brisk walking, jogging, swimming, horse riding, boxing, rock climbing or dancing, so think outside the box!

Do something
today that
your future
self will thank
you for.

Sean Patrick Flanery

Take care of
your body.
It's the only
place you
have to live.

Jim Rohn

GO FOR A WALK

The humble walk boasts a multitude of fantastic physical health benefits, including building stamina, burning calories and improving your cardiovascular health. On top of that, walking is a perfect way to ease stress and enhance positive and calming energy. A walk through green space, such as a park or woodland, or near water, such as a stream or coastal path, only serves to enhance these effects. The beauty of walking is you don't need any specialist equipment, nor do you need to be super fit to reap the rewards, making it a simple but effective way to practice self-care.

Be healthy and take
care of yourself, but
be happy with the
beautiful things that
make you, you.

Beyoncé

TRY YOGA

Yoga is a spiritual practice that focuses on uniting the mind, body and spirit (the term "yoga" is rooted in the Sanskrit *yuj*, meaning "to unite"). It blends physical postures (*asanas*) with meditation, and can help to create a sense of balance within the body, improving flexibility and strength, while also evoking a sense of peace and stillness. Yoga is for everyone, not just the super flexible, so give it a try – if you're new to yoga practice, seek out a beginner or *hatha* (slow, gentle yoga) class.

The only way to achieve
beauty is to feel it from
inside without breaking
it down into individual
physical attributes.

MILEY CYRUS

TO BE BEAUTIFUL
MEANS TO BE YOURSELF.
YOU DON'T NEED TO
BE ACCEPTED BY
OTHERS. YOU NEED
TO ACCEPT YOURSELF.

THÍCH NHẤT HẠNH

FUEL YOUR BODY WELL

Eating a healthy, balanced diet is an important act of self-care that will benefit both your body and mind. By fuelling your body correctly, you will be taking an active and positive step toward good overall health, which will see you achieve a healthy body weight, reduce your risk of developing cardiovascular disease and improve your self-esteem. When looking to eat healthily,

avoid fad diets and instead aim to eat enough protein (for example, lean meat, fish, tofu, beans, pulses and nuts), carbohydrates (for example, wholegrain bread and pasta, rice and starchy vegetables) and healthy fats (for example, avocados, oily fish, nuts and olive oil), as well as a wide variety of vitamin-rich fruits and vegetables. Start viewing food in terms of its nutritional value, to ensure you're well fuelled and energized.

TO ENSURE GOOD HEALTH;
EAT LIGHTLY, BREATHE
DEEPLY, LIVE MODERATELY,
CULTIVATE CHEERFULNESS
AND MAINTAIN AN
INTEREST IN LIFE.

WILLIAM LONDEN

Beauty is how you feel
inside, and it reflects
in your eyes. It is not
something physical.

SOPHIA LOREN

BOOST YOUR
VITAMIN B INTAKE

Ensuring you are taking on a good balance
of vitamins and minerals is vital for good
self-care, with B vitamins especially
important in helping to regulate your mood.
If you're feeling low, try boosting your intake
of B vitamins, which play an important role
in the control of tryptophan, which in turn is
key for serotonin production

– the neurotransmitter thought to contribute to feelings of well-being and happiness. B vitamins can all be found in a healthy, balanced diet, but especially in eggs, avocado, yeast extract, poultry and liver, with fortified cereals and milk alternatives offering a great source, too. So top up on these for a happiness hit!

Your diet is
a bank account.
Good food
choices are good
investments.

Bethenny Frankel

Health is not
about the weight
you lose, but about
the life you gain.

Josh Axe

DRINK MORE WATER

Ensuring you drink enough water each day to stay adequately hydrated is not just vital for your physical well-being; it may also help to reduce feelings of anxiety and fatigue, and boost mood and concentration. As well as regulating bodily functions, flushing toxins from your system and promoting healthy-looking skin and hair, several studies have demonstrated that hydration

is imperative for good mental health. All of which means that drinking plenty of water each day is one of the simplest forms of self-care there is. Current guidelines state that drinking six to eight glasses of water is best for optimum health. If you're unsure whether you're dehydrated, the best way to test is to check the colour of your urine. It should be a pale straw colour. Any darker, and you can simply reach for a glass of water to get back on track!

GOOD NUTRITION
CREATES HEALTH
IN ALL AREAS OF
OUR EXISTENCE.
ALL PARTS ARE
INTERCONNECTED.

T. COLIN CAMPBELL

Cut down on alcohol

Many people drink alcohol as a way to unwind, but when focusing on self-care it would be wise to try to cut down on alcohol as much as possible. While it's true that alcohol can initially help induce feelings of relaxation, this is short-lived and is very often outweighed by negative effects, including anxiety and disturbed sleep. Alcohol is a depressant, and regular drinking will likely leave you feeling stressed, tired and less able to cope with daily life. Cutting back on that glass of wine or bottle of beer in the evenings will help boost your sense of well-being and positivity.

CHOOSE HEALTHIER COMFORT FOODS

As well as being linked to weight gain and
an increased risk of developing diabetes,
consuming too many high-sugar or
processed foods can also negatively impact
your mental health. Scientists think the
blood sugar fluctuations and inflammation

associated with eating too many refined foods increase your risk of mood swings and depression, as well as leaving you feeling lethargic and less able to cope with stress. So say no to temptations like crisps and cake, and opt for comfort foods that nourish and fuel you instead – think hearty soups, warming stews, berry smoothies, avocados, nuts and seeds, or a few squares of dark chocolate.

Learning to *love* yourself is

like learning to *walk* – essential,

life-changing.

Vironika Tugaleva

RELAX IN THE BATH

A long soak in a warm bath at the end of a busy day is the perfect way to switch off and unwind, doing wonders for your mind, body and soul. Try adding your favourite bath oil or, if your muscles feel super tense, a scoop of magnesium sulphate flakes, to ease away aches and pains, and promote good skin health. Use your favourite bath products and, for a spot of extra luxury, light a few candles to set the soothing, restorative mood.

When you recover or discover something that nourishes your soul and brings joy, care enough about yourself to make room for it in your life.

JEAN SHINODA BOLEN

There is only one corner
of the universe you can be
certain of improving, and
that's your own self.

Aldous Huxley

EXPERIMENT WITH ESSENTIAL OILS

Essential oils are a wonderful way to combat stress and alleviate anxiety, making them perfect for a spot of simple self-care. Some of the best oils to help promote a sense of peacefulness and calm include lavender, rose, vanilla and frankincense. You can use them in a variety of ways, including inhalation or applying them directly to the skin with the aid of a carrier, such as olive oil. Try applying a few drops to a tissue and breathing in the scent for instant relief; sprinkling a little on your pillow to aid a restful night's sleep; adding a few drops to your bath for a restorative soak; or mixing with a carrier oil and massaging into the skin, to ease muscle tension.

Take a nap

Taking a nap is a fabulous way to take care of your mind and body, allowing you to rest and rejuvenate before waking to tackle the rest of your day. As our days seem to become ever busier, it's important to slow the pace occasionally – and a mid-afternoon snooze is the perfect way to do so! Taking a nap has been shown to lower tension, decreasing your chance of developing heart disease, as well as boosting afternoon productivity, increasing alertness and improving mood. Just remember to set an alarm so you don't snooze right through until dinnertime!

SELF-COMPASSION SOOTHES THE MIND LIKE A LOVING FRIEND WHO'S WILLING TO LISTEN.

CHRISTOPHER GERMER

CREATE A CALMING BEDTIME ROUTINE

The end of the day is one of the easiest times to introduce more self-care into your life, as you are less likely to be disturbed and your body will be naturally winding down after the day's activities. To ensure you have the most restful night's sleep possible, create your own nurturing and calming bedtime routine, including practices and rituals that make you feel loved, relaxed and peaceful. If possible, avoid any electronic devices in the hour leading up to bedtime, as the blue light they emit alters your levels of sleep-inducing melatonin. Instead, read a chapter of your book, rinse away the stresses of the day with your favourite facial cleanser, pop on your cosiest pyjamas, massage your hands and arms with lavender-scented body cream, and take a moment before sleep to perform a breathing meditation with the lights low. Bliss!

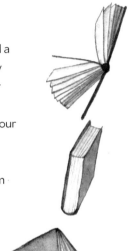

Sleep
is the best
meditation.

Anonymous

Finish each day before
you begin the next, and
interpose a solid wall of
sleep between the two.

Ralph Waldo Emerson

FEEL REVIVED BY SLEEP

Lack of sleep can impair your judgement and concentration, and increase feelings of stress and anxiety, so making sure you get enough is a critical aspect of self-care. Sleep is a vital physiological process that, over the course of the night, restores both your mind and body. Experts are in agreement that eight hours of shut-eye is about the right amount for most adults – although you will likely need to be in bed for longer to ensure you achieve that amount... perhaps nine or even ten hours. If you struggle to sleep, try implementing your relaxing bedtime routine (pp.124–125), and then aim to get into bed 15 minutes earlier every evening for a whole week. You might be amazed at the difference it makes to your energy levels and well-being.

ASK FOR SUPPORT

If you're feeling overwhelmed by a task, or feel you have
more on your plate than you can comfortably handle,
there is no shame in asking for help from others. In
fact, learning how to enlist support when you need it,
rather than striving to get everything done by yourself,
is an important component of looking after yourself.
Not only will it take the pressure off you, helping to
relieve stress, but it will also free up more of your time

to invest in replenishing your own energy. If you're not accustomed to asking for help from others, these simple steps will help: first, acknowledge you need support from someone else – accepting you have limitations is a strength, not a weakness. Next, assess exactly what you need help with, so you can figure out the best person or group to ask. Being specific will make it much easier. Next, ask! You'll be amazed at how empowering it can feel to take action by enlisting the help of another person.

A cup of tea is a cup of peace.

SEN SŌSHITSU XV

THE MORE YOU EAT, THE LESS FLAVOUR; THE LESS YOU EAT, THE MORE FLAVOUR.

CHINESE PROVERB

SAVOUR A CUP OF TEA

You might find the tension drops from your shoulders just thinking about sitting down with a hot cup of tea – and for good reason. People have relaxed over cups of tea for thousands of years – in fact, in the 1100s, formal Zen Buddhist tea-drinking ceremonies were created with the aim of aiding meditation. Studies back this up, with tea drinking shown to have similar effects on the brain as meditating, stimulating alpha brainwaves associated with deep relaxation and enhanced clarity. And – depending on the type you

drink – tea has also been shown to adjust serotonin
and dopamine levels, increasing feelings of happiness.
Bored of your regular tea? There are so many
different varieties to try: peppermint can boost
your mood and aid digestion; ginger can give you
an instant pick-me-up; and turmeric can improve
immune function, with its antioxidant, antibacterial,
antiviral and anti-inflammatory properties. So, make
time in your day to sit down and relax with a cuppa –
it will be good for your soul.

Rainy days
should be spent
at home with a
cup of tea and
a good book.

Bill Watterson

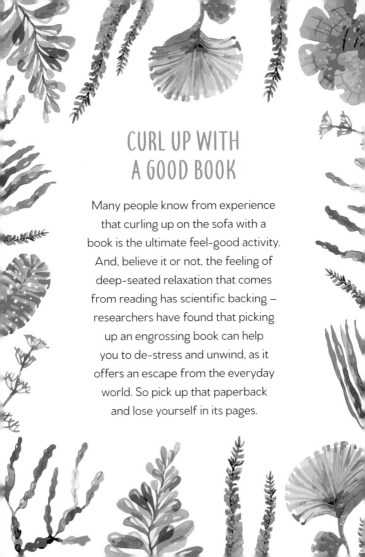

CURL UP WITH A GOOD BOOK

Many people know from experience that curling up on the sofa with a book is the ultimate feel-good activity. And, believe it or not, the feeling of deep-seated relaxation that comes from reading has scientific backing – researchers have found that picking up an engrossing book can help you to de-stress and unwind, as it offers an escape from the everyday world. So pick up that paperback and lose yourself in its pages.

*I think in life
you should work
on yourself until the
day you die.*

SERENA WILLIAMS

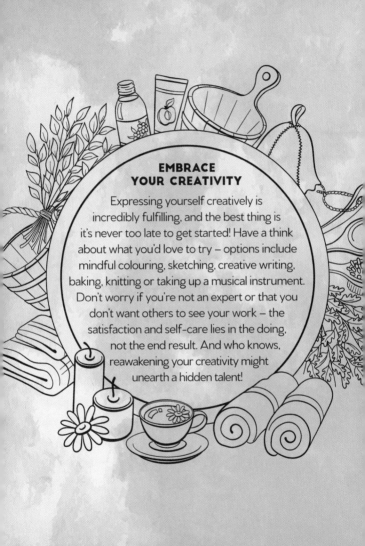

EMBRACE YOUR CREATIVITY

Expressing yourself creatively is incredibly fulfilling, and the best thing is it's never too late to get started! Have a think about what you'd love to try – options include mindful colouring, sketching, creative writing, baking, knitting or taking up a musical instrument. Don't worry if you're not an expert or that you don't want others to see your work – the satisfaction and self-care lies in the doing, not the end result. And who knows, reawakening your creativity might unearth a hidden talent!

YOU CAN'T
USE UP
CREATIVITY.
THE MORE
YOU USE,
THE MORE
YOU HAVE.

MAYA ANGELOU

NOURISHING YOURSELF
IN A WAY THAT HELPS
YOU BLOSSOM IN THE
DIRECTION YOU WANT
TO GO IS ATTAINABLE,
AND YOU ARE WORTH
THE EFFORT.

DEBORAH DAY

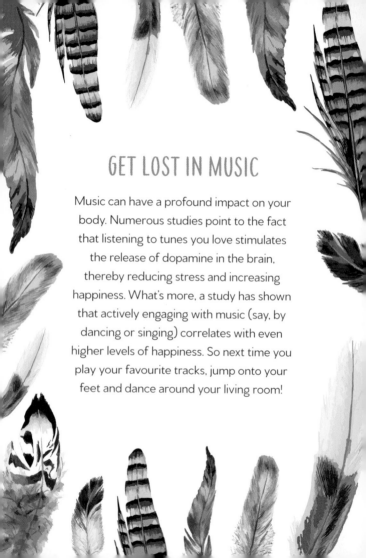

GET LOST IN MUSIC

Music can have a profound impact on your body. Numerous studies point to the fact that listening to tunes you love stimulates the release of dopamine in the brain, thereby reducing stress and increasing happiness. What's more, a study has shown that actively engaging with music (say, by dancing or singing) correlates with even higher levels of happiness. So next time you play your favourite tracks, jump onto your feet and dance around your living room!

I think *music*
in itself is *healing.*
It's an *explosive*
expression of
humanity.

Billy Joel

Work your way through your to-do list

Feeling frazzled, flustered and unable to keep up with the mounting tasks and chores that keep racing around your head? Then write them down! Creating a to-do list is a simple and effective way of freeing up your short-term memory, helping you feel calmer and more in control. Seeing your to-do list written down in black and white can make everything seem more manageable, plus being able to physically cross each task off your list once it's completed will help you feel more organized, capable and empowered. It might not seem like the most fun aspect of self-care, but it will certainly help to reduce your stress levels, which is vital for your well-being.

ASK FOR HELP,
NOT BECAUSE
YOU'RE WEAK,
BUT BECAUSE
YOU WANT TO
REMAIN STRONG.

LES BROWN

DECLUTTER YOUR HOME (OR EVEN ONE DRAWER!)

The term "self-care" might not immediately spring to mind when you think of decluttering your home but, in fact, getting rid of unwanted and unnecessary possessions can feel instantly cathartic. Clinging to material belongings and being constantly confronted with cramped cupboards and surfaces is often associated with stress. Conversely, creating a clutter-free, minimalistic living space can instantly ease your mind and promote calm. So set aside a whole day, or even just ten minutes, to declutter all or some of your home – perhaps work through just one drawer every chance you get. Don't just chuck everything in the bin – you could donate to charity shops or a local refuge centre for an added feel-good factor.

What you
put into life
is what you
get out of it.

Clint Eastwood

Love yourself
first and everything
else falls into line.
You really have
to love yourself to
get anything done
in this world.

Lucille Ball

I DON'T FOCUS ON WHAT I'M UP AGAINST. I FOCUS ON MY GOALS AND I TRY TO IGNORE THE REST.

VENUS WILLIAMS

Set yourself a new goal

Stepping outside of your comfort zone, or doing something you've dreamed of, is a simple and exciting way to boost your self-esteem. Think about a goal that sparks a fire inside of you – from signing up to drama classes or joining a book club or visiting a country you've always longed to see. Make sure it's a goal that's fully yours and not a dream that's influenced by someone else, or something you feel you "should" be excited by.

You must go on
adventures to find
out where you
truly belong.

Sue Fitzmaurice

IF YOU DON'T VALUE YOUR TIME, NEITHER WILL OTHERS.

KIM GARST

PLAN A SHORT GETAWAY

Taking a break from your usual routine is a wonderful way to switch off, relax and spend some time looking after yourself. Physically getting away from it all can be the perfect nudge to help you do this. So why not book a short break away for a night or two? You could decide to go alone, or with a friend or loved one. Spend some time seeing the sights or experiencing new things, but also try to leave some time unscheduled, where you can simply unwind. If a minibreak isn't an option for you at the moment, why not set aside a weekend to be a "tourist" in your home town? Visit somewhere nearby that's new to you (or long forgotten), sit in a café and watch the world go by, or set time aside to read an engrossing book. By simply giving yourself permission to treat a weekend at home like a weekend away, it will help you embrace that relaxed holiday vibe.

WHEN YOU ARE
COMPASSIONATE
WITH YOURSELF,
YOU TRUST IN
YOUR SOUL,
WHICH YOU
LET GUIDE
YOUR LIFE.

JOHN O'DONOHUE

CONTINUE TO
NURTURE YOURSELF

This book has hopefully given you lots of ideas and inspiration about how to care for and nourish your mind, body and soul. By continuing to include time for self-care each and every day – even if it's sometimes just for a few minutes – you will likely find yourself feeling calmer, happier and more self-assured. And always remember, if you start to feel overwhelmed, anxious or worried, just pause for a moment and take a few deep breaths, to reset your sense of calm.

IMAGE CREDITS

If you're interested in finding out more
about our books, find us on Facebook
at Summersdale Publishers and follow
us on Twitter at @Summersdale.

WWW.SUMMERSDALE.COM